50 Traditional Japanese Recipes for Home Cooks

By: Kelly Johnson

Table of Contents

- Miso Soup
- Tamagoyaki (Japanese Rolled Omelette)
- Onigiri (Rice Balls)
- Tonkatsu (Pork Cutlet)
- Teriyaki Chicken
- Tempura (Battered and Fried Seafood/Vegetables)
- Sukiyaki (Beef Hot Pot)
- Shabu-shabu (Japanese Hot Pot)
- Udon Noodles
- Soba Noodles
- Yakisoba (Stir-fried Noodles)
- Okonomiyaki (Savory Pancake)
- Takoyaki (Octopus Balls)
- Gyoza (Pan-Fried Dumplings)
- Yakitori (Grilled Chicken Skewers)
- Chawanmushi (Steamed Egg Custard)
- Oyakodon (Chicken and Egg Rice Bowl)
- Katsudon (Pork Cutlet Rice Bowl)
- Gyudon (Beef Bowl)
- Hiyayakko (Chilled Tofu)
- Niku Jaga (Meat and Potatoes Stew)
- Kinpira Gobo (Braised Burdock Root)
- Tsukemono (Japanese Pickles)
- Agedashi Tofu (Fried Tofu in Dashi Broth)
- Mentaiko Pasta (Spicy Cod Roe Pasta)
- Zaru Soba (Chilled Buckwheat Noodles)
- Sashimi (Sliced Raw Fish)
- Sushi Rolls (Maki Sushi)
- Nigiri Sushi
- Chirashizushi (Scattered Sushi)
- Inari Sushi (Tofu Pouches Stuffed with Rice)
- Nabe (Japanese Hot Pot)
- Yudofu (Tofu Hot Pot)
- Oden (Winter Hot Pot)
- Unagi Kabayaki (Grilled Eel)

- Tamago Kake Gohan (Egg Over Rice)
- Natto (Fermented Soybeans)
- Mochi (Glutinous Rice Cake)
- Anmitsu (Sweet Jelly Dessert)
- Dorayaki (Sweet Pancakes with Red Bean Filling)
- Taiyaki (Fish-shaped Cake)
- Matcha Ice Cream
- Green Tea Cake
- Mitarashi Dango (Sweet Soy Sauce Glazed Dumplings)
- Yaki Imo (Roasted Sweet Potatoes)
- Hojicha Latte (Roasted Green Tea Latte)
- Genmaicha (Brown Rice Green Tea)
- Umeshu (Plum Wine)
- Ramune (Japanese Soda)
- Melonpan (Sweet Bread with Crispy Top)

Miso Soup

Ingredients:

- 4 cups dashi (Japanese soup stock)
- 3 tbsp miso paste (white, yellow, or red)
- 1/2 cup tofu, cubed
- 1/4 cup green onions, sliced
- 1/4 cup wakame (dried seaweed), rehydrated
- Optional: mushrooms (shiitake or enoki), daikon, or carrots

Instructions:

1. Heat the dashi over medium heat, but do not let it boil.
2. In a small bowl, dissolve the miso paste with a few tablespoons of the warm dashi.
3. Slowly stir the dissolved miso into the pot of dashi.
4. Add tofu and wakame, cooking for 1-2 minutes until heated through.
5. Remove from heat and garnish with green onions before serving.

Tamagoyaki (Japanese Rolled Omelette)

Ingredients:

- 4 eggs
- 2 tbsp dashi (or water)
- 1 tbsp sugar
- 1 tsp soy sauce
- Oil for cooking

Instructions:
1. Whisk the eggs, dashi, sugar, and soy sauce in a bowl.
2. Heat a non-stick pan and lightly oil it.
3. Pour a thin layer of egg mixture into the pan.
4. Once partially set, roll the egg to one side.
5. Add more egg mixture, let it set, and roll again.
6. Repeat until all the mixture is used. Slice and serve.

Onigiri (Rice Balls)

Ingredients:

- 2 cups cooked Japanese rice
- Salt to taste
- Filling (tuna mayo, pickled plum, or grilled salmon)
- Nori (seaweed sheets)

Instructions:

1. Wet hands with water and sprinkle with salt.
2. Take a handful of rice and flatten it.
3. Place the filling in the center and shape the rice into a ball or triangle.
4. Wrap with a strip of nori and serve.

Tonkatsu (Pork Cutlet)

Ingredients:

- 4 pork cutlets
- Salt and pepper
- 1/2 cup flour
- 1 egg, beaten
- 1 cup panko breadcrumbs
- Oil for frying

Instructions:

1. Season the pork with salt and pepper.
2. Dredge in flour, dip in beaten egg, and coat with panko.
3. Heat oil in a pan and fry the cutlets until golden brown.
4. Slice and serve with Tonkatsu sauce.

Teriyaki Chicken

Ingredients:

- 2 chicken thighs (boneless, skin-on)
- 1/4 cup soy sauce
- 2 tbsp mirin
- 2 tbsp sake
- 1 tbsp sugar

Instructions:

1. Mix the soy sauce, mirin, sake, and sugar in a bowl.
2. Marinate the chicken in the sauce for 30 minutes.
3. Heat a pan and cook the chicken, skin side down, until crispy.
4. Flip and pour in the marinade, cooking until the sauce thickens.
5. Slice and serve with rice or vegetables.

Tempura (Battered and Fried Seafood/Vegetables)

Ingredients:

- 1 cup all-purpose flour
- 1 cup cold water
- 1 egg
- Seafood (shrimp, squid) or vegetables (sweet potato, bell pepper)
- Oil for frying

Instructions:
1. Mix the egg and cold water, then lightly stir in the flour to make a batter.
2. Heat oil to 350°F (180°C).
3. Dip seafood and vegetables into the batter and fry until golden.
4. Drain on paper towels and serve with tempura dipping sauce.

Sukiyaki (Beef Hot Pot)

Ingredients:

- 1 lb thinly sliced beef
- 1/4 cup soy sauce
- 1/4 cup mirin
- 1/4 cup sugar
- Vegetables (shiitake, napa cabbage, tofu)
- Cooked udon or rice (optional)

Instructions:

1. Mix soy sauce, mirin, and sugar in a pot.
2. Add beef and vegetables, simmering until cooked.
3. Serve hot, optionally with noodles or rice.

Shabu-shabu (Japanese Hot Pot)

Ingredients:

- 1 lb thinly sliced beef or pork
- Vegetables (mushrooms, spinach, napa cabbage)
- Dipping sauces (ponzu, sesame sauce)

Instructions:

1. Heat water or broth in a pot at the table.
2. Dip meat and vegetables into the broth to cook quickly.
3. Dip in sauces and enjoy.

Udon Noodles

Ingredients:

- 8 oz udon noodles
- 4 cups dashi broth
- 2 tbsp soy sauce
- 1 tbsp mirin
- Toppings (green onions, tempura, fish cake)

Instructions:

1. Cook udon noodles according to package instructions.
2. Heat dashi with soy sauce and mirin.
3. Add noodles to the broth and top with desired toppings.

Soba Noodles

Ingredients:

- 8 oz soba noodles
- 4 cups dashi broth
- 2 tbsp soy sauce
- 1 tbsp mirin
- Toppings (green onions, nori, tempura)

Instructions:

1. Cook soba noodles and rinse under cold water.
2. Heat dashi with soy sauce and mirin.
3. Serve hot or cold with desired toppings.

Yakisoba (Stir-fried Noodles)

Ingredients:

- 8 oz yakisoba noodles
- 1/2 lb pork or chicken, sliced
- Vegetables (cabbage, carrots, onions)
- Yakisoba sauce

Instructions:

1. Stir-fry meat and vegetables.
2. Add noodles and yakisoba sauce, tossing until coated.
3. Serve hot, optionally garnished with pickled ginger.

Okonomiyaki (Savory Pancake)

Ingredients:

- 1 cup flour
- 2 eggs
- 1/2 cup water
- 2 cups shredded cabbage
- Toppings (pork belly, bonito flakes, mayonnaise)

Instructions:

1. Mix flour, eggs, and water to form a batter.
2. Stir in cabbage and pour the batter onto a hot griddle.
3. Cook both sides until golden, then add toppings.

Takoyaki (Octopus Balls)

Ingredients:

- 1 cup flour
- 2 eggs
- 2 cups dashi
- Cooked octopus, diced
- Toppings (bonito flakes, mayonnaise, takoyaki sauce)
  Instructions:
1. Mix flour, eggs, and dashi to form a batter.
2. Pour batter into a heated takoyaki pan and add octopus.
3. Turn balls as they cook to achieve a round shape.
4. Serve with toppings of your choice.

Gyoza (Pan-Fried Dumplings)

Ingredients:

- 30 gyoza wrappers
- 1/2 lb ground pork
- 1/2 cup cabbage, finely chopped
- 2 green onions, chopped
- 2 tbsp soy sauce
- 1 tsp sesame oil
- Oil for frying

Instructions:

1. Mix pork, cabbage, green onions, soy sauce, and sesame oil.
2. Place a spoonful of filling in each wrapper and seal.
3. Fry dumplings until golden, then add water and cover to steam.

Yakitori (Grilled Chicken Skewers)

Ingredients:

- 1 lb chicken thighs, cut into cubes
- 1/4 cup soy sauce
- 1/4 cup mirin
- 1 tbsp sugar
- Bamboo skewers

Instructions:

1. Soak skewers in water and thread chicken onto them.
2. Mix soy sauce, mirin, and sugar.
3. Grill skewers, brushing with sauce until cooked through.

Chawanmushi (Steamed Egg Custard)

Ingredients:

- 4 eggs
- 2 cups dashi
- 2 tsp soy sauce
- 1 tsp mirin
- Toppings (chicken, shrimp, mushrooms)

Instructions:

1. Mix eggs, dashi, soy sauce, and mirin.
2. Pour into cups, adding desired toppings.
3. Steam for 15 minutes until set.

Oyakodon (Chicken and Egg Rice Bowl)

Ingredients:

- 2 chicken thighs, sliced
- 1/4 cup dashi
- 2 tbsp soy sauce
- 1 tbsp mirin
- 2 eggs, beaten
- Cooked rice

Instructions:

1. Simmer chicken with dashi, soy sauce, and mirin.
2. Pour beaten eggs over and cook until just set.
3. Serve over rice.

Katsudon (Pork Cutlet Rice Bowl)

Ingredients:

- 1 pork cutlet, breaded and fried
- 1/4 cup dashi
- 2 tbsp soy sauce
- 1 tbsp sugar
- 2 eggs, beaten
- Cooked rice

Instructions:

1. Slice the cutlet and simmer in dashi, soy sauce, and sugar.
2. Pour beaten eggs over and cook briefly.
3. Serve over rice.

Gyudon (Beef Bowl)

Ingredients:

- 1/2 lb thinly sliced beef
- 1/4 cup dashi
- 2 tbsp soy sauce
- 1 tbsp mirin
- Cooked rice

Instructions:

1. Simmer beef in dashi, soy sauce, and mirin.
2. Serve over rice with optional pickled ginger.

Hiyayakko (Chilled Tofu)

Ingredients:

- 1 block silken tofu
- Soy sauce to taste
- Toppings (green onions, bonito flakes, grated ginger)

Instructions:

1. Slice the tofu and place on a plate.
2. Drizzle with soy sauce and add desired toppings.

Niku Jaga (Meat and Potatoes Stew)

Ingredients:

- 1/2 lb thinly sliced beef
- 3 potatoes, peeled and chopped
- 1 onion, sliced
- 1/4 cup soy sauce
- 1/4 cup mirin
- 2 tbsp sugar

Instructions:

1. Sauté beef and onions until lightly browned.
2. Add potatoes, soy sauce, mirin, and sugar.
3. Simmer until potatoes are tender.

Kinpira Gobo (Braised Burdock Root)

Ingredients:

- 1 burdock root, julienned
- 1 carrot, julienned
- 2 tbsp soy sauce
- 1 tbsp mirin
- 1 tbsp sesame oil
- Sesame seeds for garnish

Instructions:

1. Heat sesame oil in a pan and stir-fry burdock and carrot until tender.
2. Add soy sauce and mirin, cooking until liquid is absorbed.
3. Garnish with sesame seeds and serve.

Tsukemono (Japanese Pickles)

Ingredients:

- 1 cucumber, sliced
- 1/2 cup rice vinegar
- 1/4 cup sugar
- 1 tsp salt
- Optional: chili flakes, daikon radish
  Instructions:
1. Mix vinegar, sugar, and salt in a bowl until dissolved.
2. Add cucumbers and any optional ingredients.
3. Refrigerate for at least 1 hour before serving.

Agedashi Tofu (Fried Tofu in Dashi Broth)

Ingredients:

- 1 block firm tofu, cubed
- 1/2 cup potato starch
- Oil for frying
- 1 cup dashi broth
- 2 tbsp soy sauce
- 1 tbsp mirin
- Toppings (green onions, bonito flakes)

Instructions:

1. Dust tofu with potato starch and fry until golden.
2. Heat dashi, soy sauce, and mirin in a pot.
3. Serve tofu in the broth and top with green onions and bonito flakes.

Mentaiko Pasta (Spicy Cod Roe Pasta)

Ingredients:

- 8 oz spaghetti
- 1/2 cup mentaiko (spicy cod roe)
- 2 tbsp butter
- 1 tbsp soy sauce
- Nori, shredded, for garnish

Instructions:

1. Cook spaghetti according to package instructions.
2. In a pan, melt butter and mix in mentaiko and soy sauce.
3. Toss cooked spaghetti in the sauce and serve with nori on top.

Zaru Soba (Chilled Buckwheat Noodles)

Ingredients:

- 8 oz soba noodles
- 1/4 cup soy sauce
- 1/4 cup mirin
- Chopped green onions and wasabi for serving

Instructions:

1. Cook soba noodles and rinse under cold water to cool.
2. Mix soy sauce and mirin in a dipping bowl.
3. Serve noodles on a bamboo mat with dipping sauce and toppings.

Sashimi (Sliced Raw Fish)

Ingredients:

- Assorted fresh fish (tuna, salmon, etc.)
- Soy sauce for dipping
- Wasabi and pickled ginger for serving
  Instructions:
1. Slice fish into thin pieces.
2. Arrange on a plate and serve with soy sauce, wasabi, and ginger.

Sushi Rolls (Maki Sushi)

Ingredients:

- 2 cups sushi rice
- 4 sheets nori
- Fillings (cucumber, avocado, crab, etc.)
- Soy sauce for dipping

Instructions:

1. Cook sushi rice and season with vinegar.
2. Spread rice on nori, add fillings, and roll tightly.
3. Slice and serve with soy sauce.

Nigiri Sushi

Ingredients:

- 2 cups sushi rice
- Assorted fish (tuna, salmon, shrimp)
- Wasabi for serving
  Instructions:
1. Cook sushi rice and season with vinegar.
2. Form small oval shapes with rice and top with fish slices.
3. Serve with wasabi on the side.

Chirashizushi (Scattered Sushi)

Ingredients:

- 2 cups sushi rice
- 1/4 cup rice vinegar
- Assorted toppings (sliced sashimi, cucumber, omelet, pickled vegetables)
- Sesame seeds for garnish

Instructions:

1. Cook sushi rice and season with rice vinegar.
2. Spread rice in a shallow dish and arrange toppings on top.
3. Garnish with sesame seeds and serve.

Inari Sushi (Tofu Pouches Stuffed with Rice)

Ingredients:

- 10 inari pouches (sweetened tofu skins)
- 2 cups sushi rice
- 1/4 cup rice vinegar
- 1 tbsp sugar
- Optional: sesame seeds or chopped vegetables for filling

Instructions:

1. Cook sushi rice and season with rice vinegar and sugar.
2. Stuff inari pouches with sushi rice, adding optional fillings if desired.
3. Serve chilled or at room temperature.

Nabe (Japanese Hot Pot)

Ingredients:

- 4 cups dashi broth
- Assorted ingredients (thinly sliced meat, vegetables, mushrooms, tofu)
- Soy sauce and mirin for seasoning
  Instructions:
1. Heat dashi in a pot and add soy sauce and mirin to taste.
2. Add assorted ingredients and cook until tender.
3. Serve hot, dipping items in ponzu sauce if desired.

Yudofu (Tofu Hot Pot)

Ingredients:

- 1 block silken tofu, cut into cubes
- 4 cups dashi broth
- Soy sauce for dipping
- Optional: chopped green onions and grated daikon

Instructions:

1. Bring dashi to a gentle simmer in a pot.
2. Add tofu cubes and cook until heated through.
3. Serve with soy sauce and toppings on the side.

Oden (Winter Hot Pot)

Ingredients:

- 6 cups dashi broth
- Assorted ingredients (daikon, boiled eggs, fish cakes, tofu)
- Soy sauce and mirin for seasoning
  Instructions:
1. Simmer dashi with soy sauce and mirin in a large pot.
2. Add assorted ingredients and cook until tender.
3. Serve hot with dipping sauce if desired.

Unagi Kabayaki (Grilled Eel)

Ingredients:

- 2 eel fillets
- 1/4 cup soy sauce
- 1/4 cup mirin
- 2 tbsp sugar
- Cooked rice for serving

Instructions:

1. Mix soy sauce, mirin, and sugar in a bowl.
2. Grill eel fillets, basting with sauce until cooked through.
3. Serve over cooked rice with additional sauce.

Tamago Kake Gohan (Egg Over Rice)

Ingredients:

- 1 cup cooked rice
- 1 egg
- Soy sauce to taste
- Optional: chopped green onions
  Instructions:
1. Place hot cooked rice in a bowl.
2. Crack a raw egg over the rice and drizzle with soy sauce.
3. Mix well and serve, adding green onions if desired.

Natto (Fermented Soybeans)

Ingredients:

- 1 package natto
- Soy sauce to taste
- Optional: chopped green onions or mustard
  Instructions:
1. Open the natto package and stir well to activate the texture.
2. Drizzle with soy sauce and mix in optional toppings if desired.
3. Serve over rice or as is.

Mochi (Glutinous Rice Cake)

Ingredients:

- 1 cup glutinous rice flour
- 1/4 cup sugar
- 1 cup water
- Cornstarch for dusting
- Optional: sweet fillings (red bean paste, strawberries)
Instructions:
1. Mix glutinous rice flour, sugar, and water in a bowl.
2. Steam the mixture for about 20 minutes until cooked.
3. Allow to cool, then shape into small balls or fill with desired fillings. Dust with cornstarch to prevent sticking.

Anmitsu (Sweet Jelly Dessert)

Ingredients:

- 1 cup agar-agar, cut into cubes
- 2 cups water
- 1/2 cup red bean paste
- Fresh fruits (melon, strawberries, oranges)
- Sweet syrup (e.g., honey or sugar syrup)

Instructions:

1. Dissolve agar-agar in boiling water and let it cool until set.
2. Cut into cubes and arrange with red bean paste and fresh fruits.
3. Drizzle with sweet syrup before serving.

Dorayaki (Sweet Pancakes with Red Bean Filling)

Ingredients:

- 1 cup all-purpose flour
- 2/3 cup sugar
- 1/2 tsp baking powder
- 2 eggs
- 1/2 cup water
- 1 cup red bean paste

Instructions:

1. Mix flour, sugar, baking powder, eggs, and water to form a batter.
2. Pour batter onto a hot griddle to form small pancakes, cooking until bubbles form.
3. Fill one pancake with red bean paste and top with another pancake to create a sandwich.

Taiyaki (Fish-shaped Cake)

Ingredients:

- 1 cup all-purpose flour
- 1/2 cup sugar
- 1 tsp baking powder
- 1 egg
- 1 cup water
- 1 cup red bean paste or other fillings (chocolate, custard)

Instructions:

1. Mix flour, sugar, baking powder, egg, and water to form a batter.
2. Preheat a taiyaki mold and pour in batter to fill half the mold.
3. Add filling, cover with more batter, and close the mold to cook until golden brown.

Matcha Ice Cream

Ingredients:

- 2 cups heavy cream
- 1 cup milk
- 3/4 cup sugar
- 2 tbsp matcha powder
- 1 tsp vanilla extract

Instructions:

1. Whisk together heavy cream, milk, sugar, matcha powder, and vanilla until smooth.
2. Pour the mixture into an ice cream maker and churn according to the manufacturer's instructions.
3. Freeze until firm before serving.

Green Tea Cake

Ingredients:

- 1 cup all-purpose flour
- 1/2 cup sugar
- 1 tsp baking powder
- 1/2 cup milk
- 1/4 cup vegetable oil
- 2 tbsp matcha powder
- 2 eggs

Instructions:

1. Preheat the oven to 350°F (175°C).
2. Mix flour, sugar, baking powder, and matcha powder in a bowl.
3. In another bowl, whisk together milk, oil, and eggs. Combine wet and dry ingredients, then pour into a cake pan.
4. Bake for 25-30 minutes until a toothpick comes out clean.

Mitarashi Dango (Sweet Soy Sauce Glazed Dumplings)

Ingredients:

- 1 cup glutinous rice flour
- 1/4 cup sugar
- 1/2 cup water
- 1/4 cup soy sauce
- 1/4 cup sugar (for glaze)

Instructions:

1. Mix glutinous rice flour, sugar, and water to form a dough.
2. Shape into small balls and boil until they float.
3. In a separate pan, mix soy sauce and sugar, then cook until syrupy.
4. Skewer the dumplings and brush with the glaze before serving.

Yaki Imo (Roasted Sweet Potatoes)

Ingredients:

- 2 medium sweet potatoes
- Optional: salt or butter for serving
  Instructions:
1. Preheat the oven to 400°F (200°C).
2. Wash and dry sweet potatoes, then pierce the skin with a fork.
3. Place on a baking sheet and roast for 45-60 minutes until tender.
4. Serve warm, optionally with salt or butter.

Hojicha Latte (Roasted Green Tea Latte)

Ingredients:

- 2 tbsp hojicha powder
- 1 cup milk (dairy or plant-based)
- 1 tbsp sweetener (sugar, honey, or syrup)
- Optional: whipped cream for topping
  Instructions:
1. Whisk hojicha powder and sweetener with a small amount of hot water until smooth.
2. Heat milk until hot but not boiling, then froth if desired.
3. Combine the hojicha mixture with milk and top with whipped cream if using.

Genmaicha (Brown Rice Green Tea)

Ingredients:

- 2 cups water
- 1-2 tbsp genmaicha tea leaves
  Instructions:
1. Boil water and let it cool slightly (about 175°F or 80°C).
2. Add genmaicha tea leaves to the water and steep for 2-3 minutes.
3. Strain the tea leaves and serve hot.

Umeshu (Plum Wine)

Ingredients:

- 500g ume (Japanese plums)
- 500g sugar
- 1 liter shochu or vodka
  Instructions:
1. Wash ume and dry thoroughly.
2. In a jar, layer ume with sugar, then pour in shochu or vodka.
3. Seal the jar and let it sit in a cool, dark place for at least 6 months, shaking occasionally.

Ramune (Japanese Soda)

Ingredients:

- 1 cup sugar
- 1 cup water
- 1/4 cup lemon juice
- 1/4 tsp food flavoring (like melon, strawberry, or other flavors)
- Carbonated water

Instructions:

1. In a saucepan, heat sugar and water until dissolved.
2. Remove from heat and add lemon juice and food flavoring.
3. Let it cool, then mix with carbonated water to taste before serving.

Melonpan (Sweet Bread with Crispy Top)

Ingredients:

- 2 cups bread flour
- 1/2 cup sugar
- 1/2 cup milk
- 1/4 cup butter, softened
- 1 egg
- 1 tsp yeast
- 1/2 tsp salt
- 1 cup cookie dough (for topping)

Instructions:

1. Mix bread flour, sugar, milk, butter, egg, yeast, and salt to form a dough.
2. Let the dough rise until doubled in size, about 1 hour.
3. Shape into balls, then top with cookie dough.
4. Bake at 350°F (175°C) for 15-20 minutes until golden brown.